Blue and Magenta are making **word family** pictures for a school project. Will you help them make pictures for Miss Marigold's Word Family Wall?

You'll need the special decoder wand included in this book. Use it to see the answers hidden next to Blue's pawprints.

Blue and Magenta want to start with the **at** word family. Words in the **at** family rhyme with **pat**. Can you find three things whose names belong to the **at** family? Circle them.

Shhh! Periwinkle is taking a **nap**. **Nap** belongs to the **ap** word family. Will you help Magenta and Blue look for other things whose names belong to the **ap** word family? Circle two things that rhyme with **nap** and use the decoder to check your answers.

Look! Paprika and Cinnamon are playing with Blue's toy **van**. Blue wants pictures of other things whose names end in **an**.

Do you see three other things that belong to the **an** word family? Circle them. Use the decoder to check your answers.

Tickety can help sort the word family pictures Blue and Magenta have collected so far. Will you help too? Write the word family ending for each group of pictures.

ap	at	an

Now Blue and Magenta are trying to **spot** things that belong to the **ot** family. Words in the **ot** family rhyme with **spot**.

Do you **spot** three more things that end with the sound of **ot**? Circle them.

Hop! Hop! Hop! Purple Kangaroo is so excited! He is helping Blue and Magenta find things for the **op** word family photos! Words in the **op** family rhyme with **hop**.

Will you help him figure out which things to choose? Circle three things whose names end with **op**.

Magenta had a great idea! She wrote a rhyme about the **og** word family.

Read the rhyme and circle all the pictures of things whose names end with **og** .

and **went for a jog.**

They saw a little pink pig and a big pink  **.**

They passed a  **and saw a**  **.**

On top of the  **was a little green**  **.**

Pail and Shovel can help sort more pictures. Will you help, too? Say the name of each picture. Then draw a line to match the first letter in its name with the correct word family ending.

 l	op
 m	og
 p	op
 h	ot
 t	og

Blue is cutting out pictures from magazines and circling the part that shows something whose name belongs to the **ip** word family. She circled the **tip** of the pencil. Say the name of everything you see in each picture. Circle three things whose names end in **ip**.

Magenta is cutting out pictures, too. She is circling things that belong to the **in** word family, like the pumpkin's big **grin**. Will you help Magenta? Say the name of everything you see in each picture. Circle three things whose names end in **in**.

Use the decoder to check your answers.

Blue is giving Green Puppy a great big **hug** because she found things for Blue's **ug** family pictures. **Hug** belongs to the **ug** word family.

Find and circle three things Green Puppy picked out for the **ug** word family picture.

Blue and Magenta asked their friends for help with the **um** word family pictures.

Find and circle two things whose names end in **um**. Then circle the friend who is doing something that ends in **um**.

Slippery Soap wants to sort these pictures for Blue and Magenta's project. Say the name of each picture. Then draw a line to match the first part of its name with the correct word family ending.

	**b** - - - - - - - - - - - - - - - - -	**ug**
	**sh**	**um**
	**dr**	**ug**
	**r**	**in**
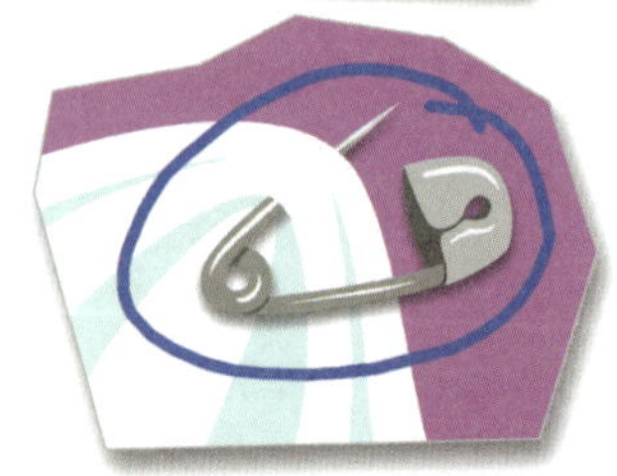	**p**	**ip**

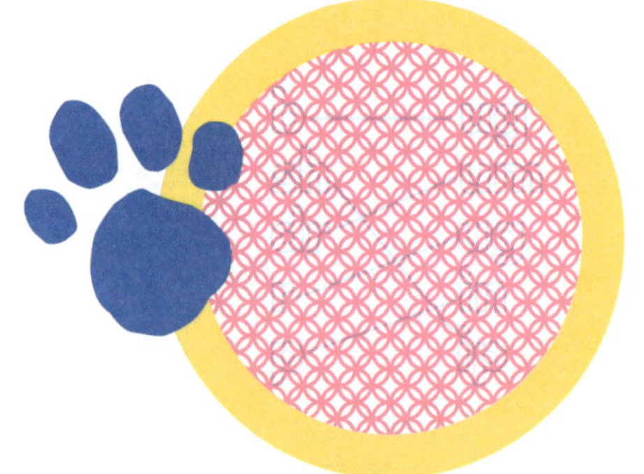

Magenta and Blue are in the **den** looking for things for the **en** word family picture. **Den** belongs to the **en** word family.

Circle three things you see whose names end with **en**. Don't forget to use your decoder to check your answers!

Magenta wants to take an **ell** family photo. Periwinkle is helping her get ready. Will you help him by circling three things whose names end in **ell?**

Click! Magenta is taking **ick** word family photos! **Click** belongs to the **ick** word family.

Which two things should Magenta take pictures of? Circle them.

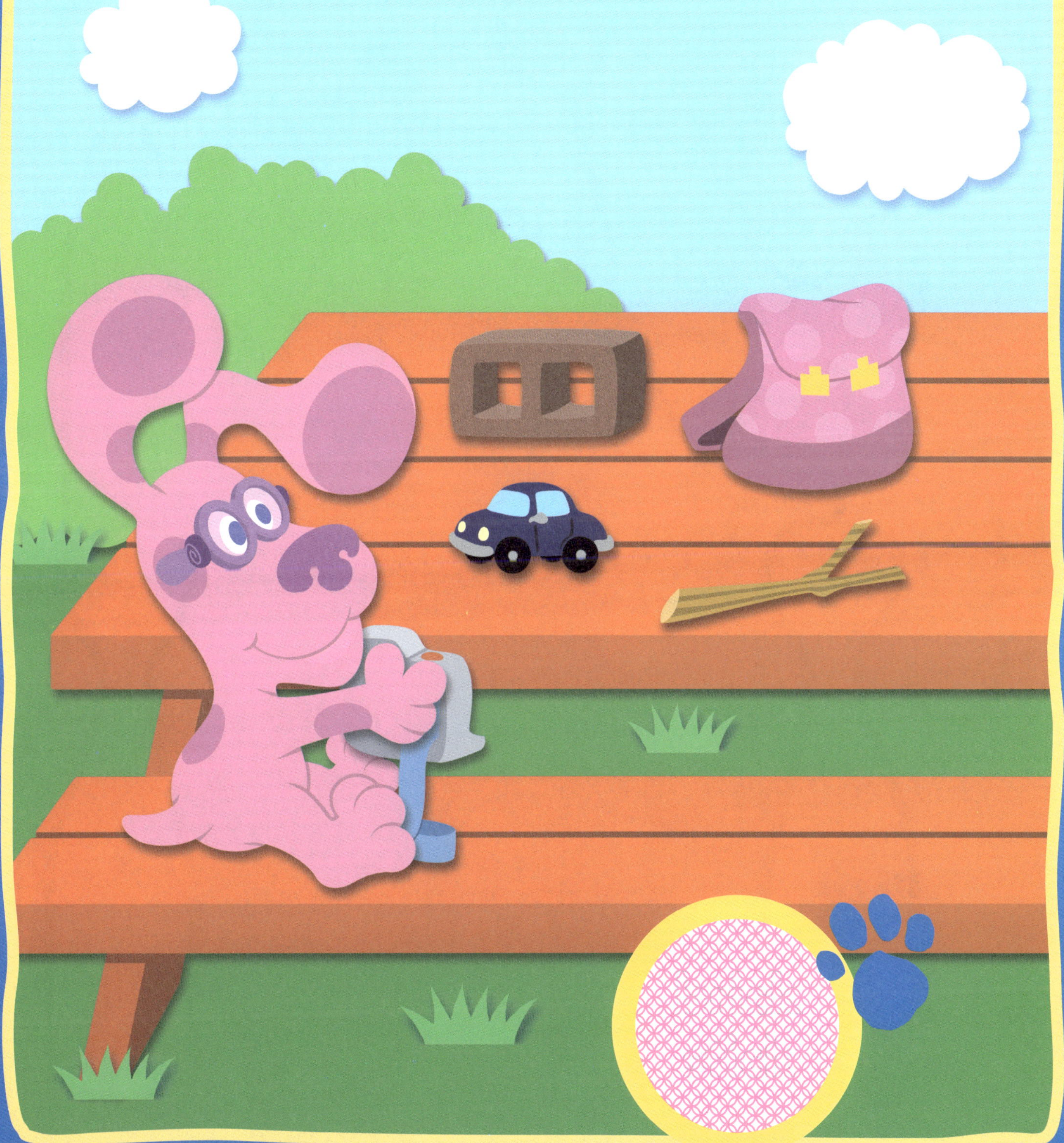

Tickety Tock is a clock, so Blue is drawing her friend for an **ock** word family picture. **Tock** and **clock** both end with the sound of **ock**.

What other things should Blue draw? Circle three things whose names belong to the **ock** word family.

Mr. Salt and Mrs. Pepper can help Blue and Magenta sort their pictures, but they need help remembering the word ending that goes with each picture.

Use the word endings in the box to finish writing the name of each object.

en	**ell**	**ick**	**ock**

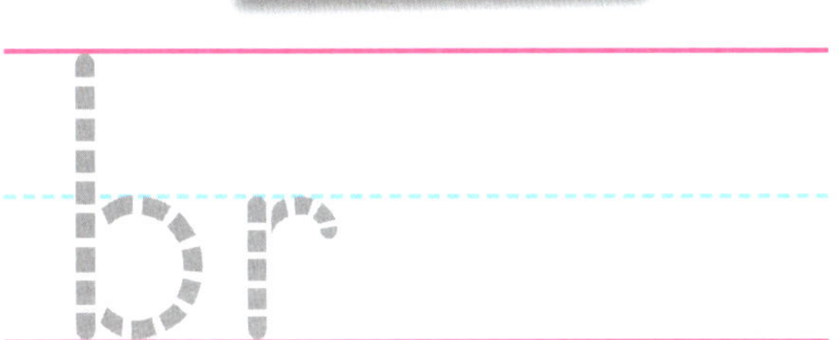

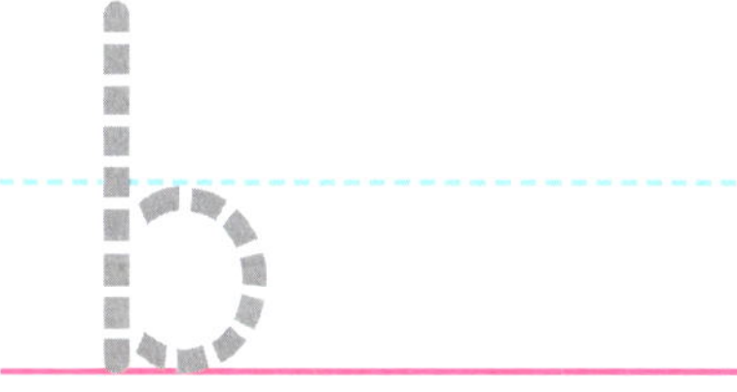

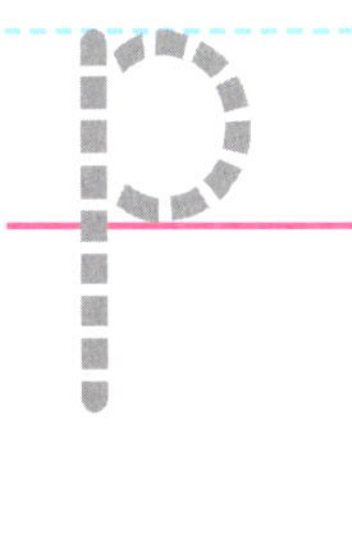

Blue and Magenta have glued all their pictures onto poster paper. Now they have to put the correct word family name with each group of pictures. Circle the correct word family ending for each group.

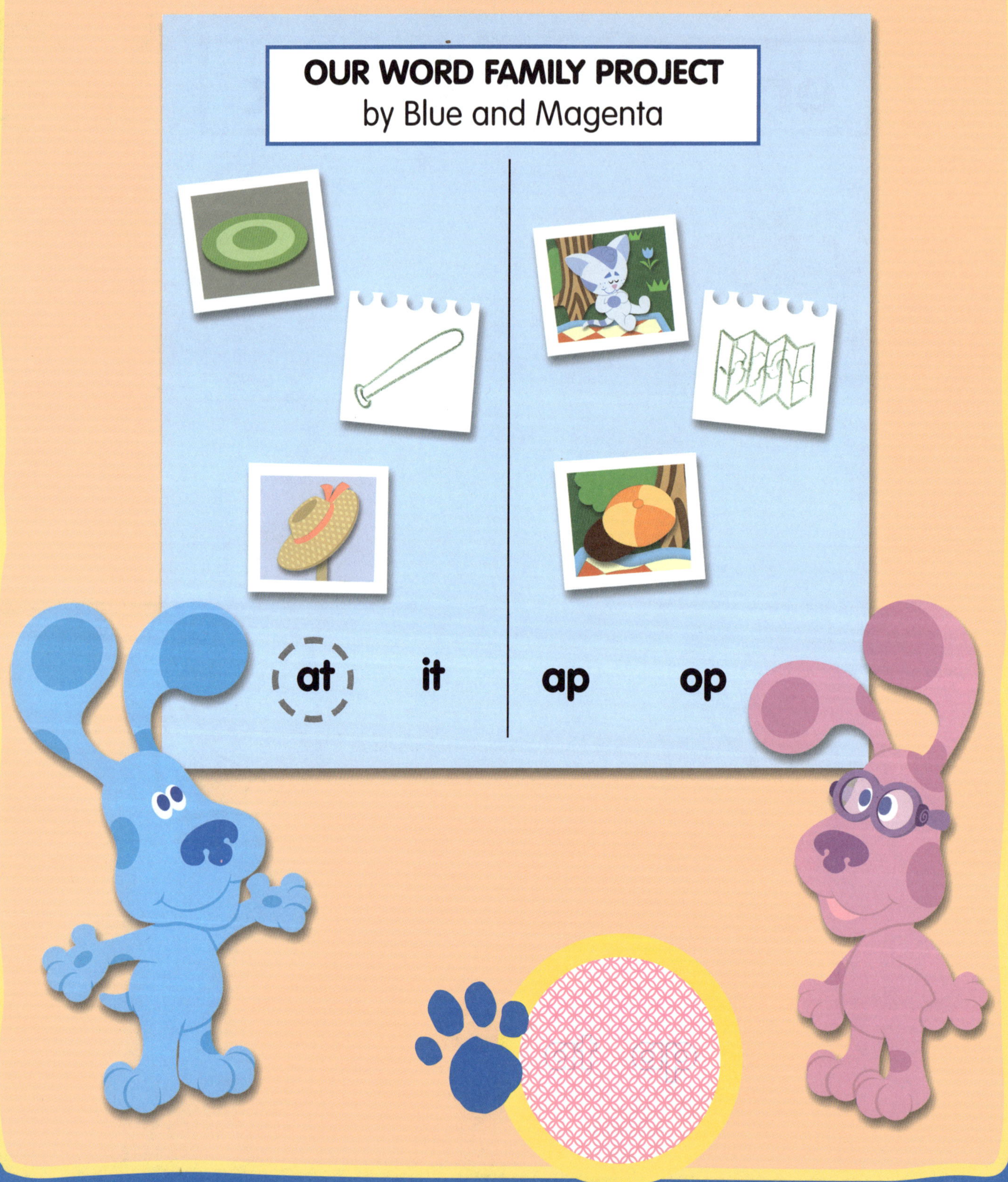

Circle the correct word family ending for each group of pictures.
Use your decoder to check your answers

Circle the correct word family ending for each group of pictures.

Circle the correct word family ending for each group of pictures.

en in	ell en
ock ick	ock ick

Look! Miss Marigold's Word Family Wall is almost finished. But a few of the pictures fell off their posters. Will you draw a line from each picture to the place where it belongs?

Great job! Thanks for all your help.